Pilots

by Fran Hodgkins

Consultant:
Thomas Haines, pilot
Editor-in-Chief
Aircraft Owners and Pilots Association

Bridgestone Books
an imprint of Capstone Press
Mankato, Minnesota

Bridgestone Books are published by Capstone Press
151 Good Counsel Drive, P.O. Box 669, Mankato, Minnesota 56002
http://www.capstone-press.com

Library of Congress Cataloging-in-Publication Data
Hodgkins, Fran, 1964–
    Pilots/by Fran Hodgkins.
    p. cm.—(Community helpers)
    Includes bibliographical references (p. 24) and index.
    ISBN 0-7368-0810-8
    1. Air pilots—Juvenile literature. [1. Air pilots. 2. Occupations.] I. Title. II. Community
helpers (Mankato, Minn.)
TL547 .H617 2001
629.13′092—dc21
                  00-009666

Summary: A simple introduction to the work pilots do, the tools they use, necessary
    schooling, and their importance to the communities they serve.

Editorial Credits
Sarah Lynn Schuette, editor; Karen Risch, product planning editor; Heather Kindseth,
    cover designer; Timothy Halldin, illustrator; Heidi Schoof, photo researcher

Photo Credits
David F. Clobes, 4, 6, 16
David R. Frazier Photolibrary, 14
James L. Shaffer, 10
K. D. Dittlinger, 18
Matt Brown/Pictor, cover
Photo Network/Jeff Greenberg, 12
Photri Inc./Bill Barley, 20
Visuals Unlimited/Steve Strickland, 8

1 2 3 4 5 6 06 05 04 03 02 01

Table of Contents

Pilots

Pilots fly aircraft. Some pilots fly large airplanes that transport people and cargo. These pilots may fly thousands of miles in one trip. Other pilots fly airplanes for fun.

transport
to move something from
one place to another

What Pilots Do

Pilots control an aircraft's take-off, flight, and landing. Pilots plan the best route to take. They check weather reports to make sure flights will be safe.

route
the course a person follows to get from one place to another

7

Different Kinds of Aircraft

Pilots fly different kinds of aircraft. They fly small private planes or jets. Pilots also fly helicopters and military planes. Many pilots fly large airliners and cargo planes.

military

the armed forces of a country

Airports

Most pilots take off and land their planes at airports. Airports have control towers. Planes drive on a taxiway to get to a runway. The runway is a strip of flat land where planes take off and land. Planes are parked in hangars when they are not flying.

control tower

a tall building where people schedule take-offs and landings at an airport

Tools Pilots Use

Pilots use the controls in a cockpit to fly planes. Controls help the pilot steer and turn the plane. Gauges tell how high and how fast the plane is flying. Other instruments show how the engines are working.

cockpit

the area in the front of a plane where the pilot sits

What Pilots Wear

Some pilots who fly for airlines wear uniforms. Pilots also wear headsets. This tool helps pilots hear directions from the control tower. Pilots talk to the control tower through a microphone on the headset.

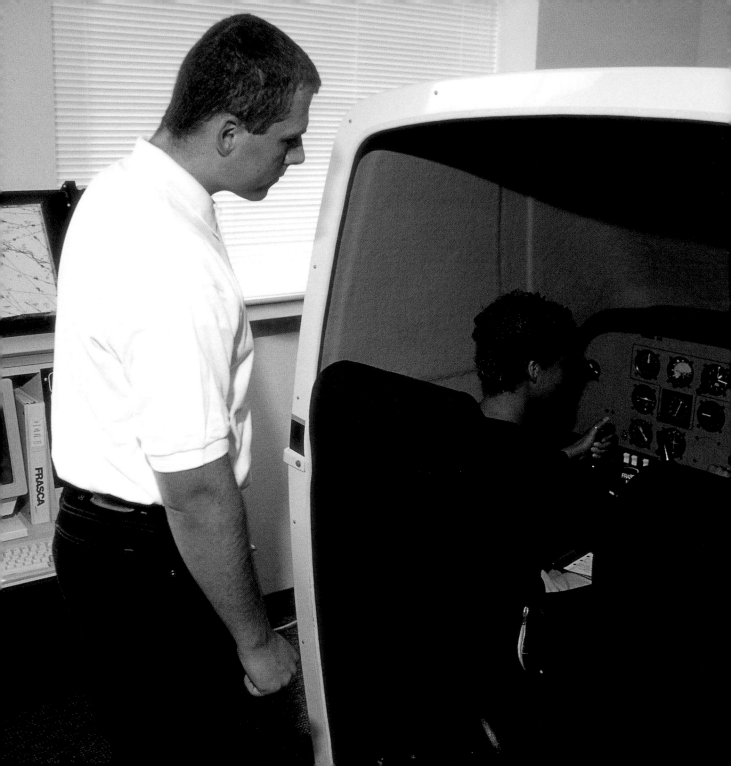

Pilots and School

Some people learn how to fly aircraft in the military. Other people go to flight school. They must take a written test and pass a flying exam. Pilots then earn a certificate. This piece of paper proves that a pilot has had the right training.

People Who Help Pilots

Many people help pilots. Mechanics make sure aircraft are working correctly. Air traffic controllers tell pilots when it is safe to take off and to land. Cargo handlers move luggage or cargo into and out of a plane. Flight attendants keep passengers safe and comfortable.

mechanic

a person who fixes machines; mechanics often fix helicopters and other aircraft.

How Pilots Help Others

Some pilots fly helicopters that take people to the hospital quickly. Other pilots use their planes to help farmers spray their crops to kill bugs and weeds. Airline pilots often fly planes to other countries. Pilots transport people and cargo all over the world.

Hands On: Make a Paper Airplane

You can make your own paper airplane. You will need an 8.5-inch by 11-inch (22-centimeter by 28-centimeter) piece of paper, stapler, and markers for this activity. Follow the instructions and diagrams below to make your paper airplane.

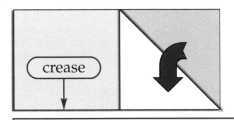 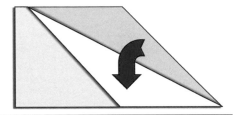

Fold the paper in half the long way and make a crease. Now, fold the top right corner of the paper down. Flip the paper over and repeat on the other side. Next, fold the diagonal edge down. Repeat on the other side. These folds will make a long edge.

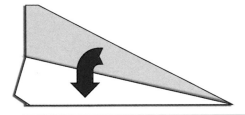 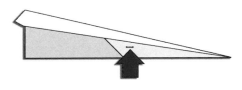

Fold the long edge down. Flip the paper over and repeat on the other side. Grasp your plane on the middle crease. Open the flaps so they look like wings. Staple the middle crease to hold the folds together. Use the markers to decorate your paper airplane.

Words to Know

cargo (KAR-goh)—the goods people use

gauges (GAY-jiz)—the instruments used to measure information such as speed

hangar (HANG-ur)—a large building where airplanes are parked

helicopter (HEL-uh-kop-tur)—an aircraft that can take off and land in a small space

instruments (IN-struh-muhnts)—the tools used to fly an airplane

microphone (MYE-kruh-fone)—an instrument used to make sound louder

runway (RUHN-way)—a strip of level land; airplanes use runways to take off and land.

taxiway (TAK-see-way)—a road that leads to the runway

Read More

Schaefer, Lola M. *Airplanes.* Transportation Library. Mankato, Minn.: Bridgestone Books, 2000.

Schomp, Virginia. *If You Were a Pilot.* New York: Benchmark Books, 1999.

Internet Sites

Amelia's Airplane Hangar
http://www.dot.gov/edu/k5/airplane.htm
Off to a Flying Start
http://k12unix.larc.nasa.gov/flyingstart/module1.html
Pilot
http://stats.bls.gov:80/k12/html/sci_005.htm
Plane Math
http://www.planemath.com/activities/pmactivities4.html

Index